CHRISTMAS FAVORITES

Solos and Band Arrangements
Correlated with Essential Elements Band Method

ARRANGED BY
MICHAEL SWEENEY

Welcome to Essential Elements Christmas Favorites! There are two versions of each holiday selection in this versatile book:

1. The SOLO version (with lyrics) appears on the left-hand page.
2. The FULL BAND arrangement appears on the right-hand page.

Use the optional accompaniment tape when playing solos for friends and family. Your director may also use the accompaniment tape in band rehearsals and concerts.

ISBN 978-0-7935-1751-0

HAL•LEONARD®
CORPORATION

7777 W. BLUEMOUND RD. P.O. BOX 13819 MILWAUKEE, WI 53213

00862500

JINGLE BELLS

Words and Music by J. PIERPONT
Arranged by MICHAEL SWEENEY

Solo

JINGLE BELLS

Words and Music by J. PIERPONT
Arranged by MICHAEL SWEENEY

Band Arrangement

00862500

UP ON THE HOUSETOP

Arranged by MICHAEL SWEENEY

Solo

UP ON THE HOUSETOP

Band Arrangement

Arranged by MICHAEL SWEENEY

Moderately fast

THE HANUKKAH SONG

Arranged by MICHAEL SWEENEY

Solo

THE HANUKKAH SONG

Band Arrangement

Arranged by MICHAEL SWEENEY

00862500

A HOLLY JOLLY CHRISTMAS

Music and Lyrics by JOHNNY MARKS
Arranged by MICHAEL SWEENEY

Solo

Lyrics under the staves:

Have a hol-ly jol-ly Christ-mas, it's the best time of the year. I don't know if there'll be snow but have a cup of cheer. Have a hol-ly jol-ly Christ-mas, and when you walk down the street Say hel-lo to friends you know and ev-'ry-one you meet. Oh, ho, the mis-tle-toe hung where you can see. Some-bod-y waits for you. Kiss her once for me. Have a hol-ly jol-ly Christ-mas, and in case you did-n't hear, Oh, by gol-ly have a hol-ly jol-ly Christ-mas this year. Christ-mas this year.

A HOLLY JOLLY CHRISTMAS

Music and Lyrics by JOHNNY MARKS
Arranged by MICHAEL SWEENEY

Band Arrangement

WE WISH YOU A MERRY CHRISTMAS

Solo

Arranged by MICHAEL SWEENEY

WE WISH YOU A MERRY CHRISTMAS

Band Arrangement

Arranged by MICHAEL SWEENEY

00862500

FROSTY THE SNOW MAN

Words and Music by STEVE NELSON and JACK ROLLINS
Arranged by MICHAEL SWEENEY

Solo

Frosty The Snow Man

Words and Music by STEVE NELSON and JACK ROLLINS

Arranged by MICHAEL SWEENEY

Band Arrangement

ROCKIN' AROUND THE CHRISTMAS TREE

Music and Lyrics by JOHNNY MARKS
Arranged by MICHAEL SWEENEY

Solo

Introduction

Rock-in' a-round the Christ-mas tree _ at the Christ-mas par-ty
Rock-in' a-round the Christ-mas tree _ let the Christ-mas spir-it

hop. Mis-tle-toe hung where you can see _ ev-'ry cou-ple tries to
ring. Lat-er we'll have some pump-kin pie _ and we'll

stop. do some car-ol-ing. You will get a sen-ti-men-tal feel-ing when you

hear voic-es sing-ing, "Let's be jol-ly, Deck the halls with

boughs of hol-ly." Rock-in' a-round the Christ-mas tree. _ Have a

hap-py hol-i-day. Ev-'ry-one danc-ing mer-ri-ly _ in the

new old fash-ioned way. Rock-in' a-round the Christ-mas tree. _ Have a

hap-py hol-i-day. Ev-'ry-one danc-ing mer-ri-ly _ in the

new old fash-ioned way. _____

ROCKIN' AROUND THE CHRISTMAS TREE

Music and Lyrics by JOHNNY MARKS
Arranged by MICHAEL SWEENEY

Band Arrangement

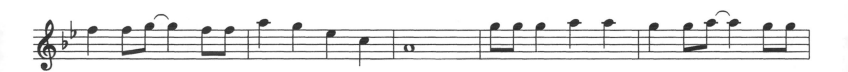

00862500

JINGLE-BELL ROCK

Words and Music by JOE BEAL and JIM BOOTHE
Arranged by MICHAEL SWEENEY

Solo

Jin-gle-bell, Jin-gle-bell, Jin-gle-bell rock Jin-gle-bell swing and Jin-gle-bells ring. Snow-in' and blow-in' up bush-els of fun Now the Jin-gle-hop has be-gun. Jin-gle-bell, Jin-gle-bell, Jin-gle-bell rock Jin-gle-bells chime in Jin-gle-bell time. Danc-in' and pranc-in' in Jin-gle-bell Square In the frost-y air. What a bright time, it's the right time to rock the night a-way. Jin-gle-bell time is a swell time to go glid-in' in a one-horse sleigh. Gid-dy-ap, Jin-gle-horse pick up your feet. Jin-gle a-round the clock. Mix and min-gle in a jin-gl-in' beat. That's the Jin-gle-bell, That's the Jin-gle-bell, That's the Jin-gle-bell rock.

00862500

JINGLE-BELL ROCK

**Words and Music by JOE BEAL
and JIM BOOTHE**
Arranged by MICHAEL SWEENEY

Band Arrangement

RUDOLPH THE RED-NOSED REINDEER

Music and Lyrics by JOHNNY MARKS
Arranged by MICHAEL SWEENEY

Solo **Introduction - Moderately Slow**

You know Dash-er and Danc-er and Pranc-er and Vix-en, Com-et and Cu-pid and Don-ner and Blitz-en, but do you re-call the most fa-mous rein-deer of all.

11 Moderate Bossa

Ru-dolph, the red-nosed rein-deer had a ver-y shin-y nose, and if you ev-er saw it, you would e-ven say it glows. All of the oth-er rein-deer used to laugh and call him names, they nev-er let poor Ru-dolph join in an-y rein-deer games. Then one fog-gy Christ-mas Eve, San-ta came to say, "Ru-dolph, with your nose so bright, won't you guide my sleigh to-night?" Then how the rein-deer loved him as they shout-ed out with glee: "Ru-dolph, the red-nosed rein-deer, you'll go down in his-to-ry!" you'll go down in his-to-ry!"

RUDOLPH THE RED-NOSED REINDEER

Music and Lyrics by JOHNNY MARKS
Arranged by MICHAEL SWEENEY

Band Arrangement

LET IT SNOW!
LET IT SNOW! LET IT SNOW!

Words by SAMMY CAHN
Music by JULE STYNE
Arranged by MICHAEL SWEENEY

Solo

Oh the weath-er out-side is fright-ful But the fire is so de-light-ful, And since we've no place to go, Let it snow! Let it snow! Let it snow! It does-n't show signs of stop-ping, And I brought some corn for pop-ping, The lights are turned way down low, Let it snow! Let it snow! Let it snow! When we fi-nal-ly kiss good-night, How I'll hate go-ing out in the storm! But if you'll real-ly hold me tight, All the way home I'll be warm. The fire is slow-ly dy-ing And my dear we're still good-bye-ing, But as long as you love me so, Let it snow! Let it snow! Let it snow! When we snow!

LET IT SNOW! LET IT SNOW! LET IT SNOW!

Words by SAMMY CAHN
Music by JULE STYNE
Arranged by MICHAEL SWEENEY

Band Arrangement

00862500

THE CHRISTMAS SONG

Music and Lyric by MEL TORME and ROBERT WELLS

Arranged by MICHAEL SWEENEY

Solo

Chest-nuts roast-ing on an o-pen fire, Jack Frost nip-ping at your nose, Yule-tide carols be-ing sung by a choir and folks dressed up like Es-ki-mos. Ev-'ry-bod-y knows a tur-key and some mis-tle-toe help to make the sea-son bright. Ti-ny tots with their eyes all a-glow will find it hard to sleep to-night. They know that San-ta's on his way; He's load-ed lots of toys and good-ies on his sleigh. And ev-'ry moth-er's child __ is gon-na spy to see if reindeer real-ly know how to fly. And so I'm of-fer-ing this sim-ple phrase to kids from one to nine-ty-two. Al-tho' it's been said man-y times, man-y ways: "Mer-ry Christ-mas, Mer-ry Christ-mas, Mer-ry Christ-mas __ to you."

THE CHRISTMAS SONG

Music and Lyric by MEL TORME and ROBERT WELLS
Arranged by MICHAEL SWEENEY

Band Arrangement

00862500